TABLE OF CONTENTS

EXECUTIVE SUMMARY

Gender equality and female empowerment are core development objectives, fundamental for the realization of human rights and key to effective and sustainable development outcomes. No society can develop successfully without providing equitable opportunities, resources, and life prospects for males and females so that they can shape their own lives and contribute to their families and communities. Although many gender gaps have narrowed over the past two decades, substantial inequalities remain across all sectors in which USAID works, particularly in low-income and conflict-affected countries and among disadvantaged groups.

USAID has a long history of supporting programming to increase gender equality. Over the past two years alone, changes to the Automated Directives System (ADS), revised technical competencies required for Foreign Service backstops, new definitions of gender issues for budget attribution, new senior positions devoted exclusively to gender equality and female empowerment, and new common indicators to measure progress in this arena have strengthened the Agency's ability to address key gender issues and track our progress in doing so. Still, an updated Agency policy on gender equality and female empowerment is needed to reflect fundamental changes in the world and the evidence that has accumulated since the 1982 Policy Paper on Women in Development was issued. This new policy on Gender Equality and Female Empowerment builds on the Agency's progress to date.

The goal of this policy is to improve the lives of citizens around the world by advancing equality between females and males, and empowering women and girls to participate fully in and benefit from the development of their societies. It will be addressed through integration of gender equality and female empowerment throughout the Agency's Program Cycle and related processes: in strategic planning, project design and implementation, and monitoring and evaluation. This integrated approach positions the Agency to address gender gaps and the constraints that hold women back.

Under this policy, USAID investments are aimed at three overarching outcomes. In strategic planning at the country or project level, these outcomes will be adapted and translated into specific results with associated targets and indicators. These outcomes, which are especially important for people who are marginalized or excluded due to ethnicity, gender identity, sexual orientation, lack of income, disability or other factors, reflect the gamut of activities that USAID undertakes across multiple sectors and fields:

- Reduce gender disparities in access to, control over and benefit from resources, wealth, opportunities and services - economic, social, political, and cultural;

- Reduce gender-based violence and mitigate its harmful effects on individuals and communities; and

- Increase capability of women and girls to realize their rights, determine their life outcomes, and influence decision-making in households, communities, and societies.

Seven guiding principles underpin this policy, reflecting key features of the USAID Policy Framework 2011-2015 and the parameters of the USAID Forward reform agenda:

- **_Integrate gender equality and female empowerment into USAID's work:_** This policy will be implemented by integrating approaches and actions to advance gender equality and female empowerment throughout the Agency's Program Cycle. USAID will also make strategic investments to promote gender equality and female empowerment.

- **Pursue an inclusive approach to foster equality:** This policy is inclusive of all women and men, girls and boys, regardless of age, sexual orientation, gender identity, disability status, religion, ethnicity, socioeconomic status, geographic area, migratory status, forced displacement or HIV/AIDS status.

- **Build partnerships across a wide range of stakeholders:** USAID will partner with host governments, civil society, the private sector and other donors to ensure that our efforts are coordinated and non-duplicative, build on the skills and initiatives of local actors, and reflect country priorities.

- **Harness science, technology, and innovation to reduce gender gaps and empower women and girls:** USAID investments should make bold and imaginative use of new technologies to change discriminatory social norms and stereotypes, and empower women and girls to wield greater influence in society.

- **Address the unique challenges in crisis and conflict-affected environments:** USAID's work in conflict-affected and fragile states should promote women's participation in all efforts to prevent, resolve and rebuild following conflict; prevent and respond to sexual and gender based violence; and ensure that relief and recovery efforts address the different needs and priorities of women and men.

- **Serve as a thought-leader and a learning community:** The Agency will measure performance in closing key gender gaps and empowering women and girls, learn from successes and failures and disseminate best practices on gender integration throughout the Agency.

- **Hold ourselves accountable:** Gender equality and female empowerment is a shared Agency responsibility and depends on the contribution and collective commitment of all staff, with particular emphasis on senior managers and Mission Directors.

This policy applies to all bureaus and missions and covers policy and programmatic operations in Washington and the field. The policy includes detailed descriptions of organizational roles and responsibilities to institutionalize the policy in missions, regional bureaus, pillar bureaus, the Office of Gender Equality and Women's Empowerment, the Office of Acquisition and Assistance, the Office of Human Resources, the Bureau for Policy, Planning and Learning, and the Office of the Administrator. The release of the policy will be followed by Frequently Asked Questions and Implementation Guidance, including a timetable for phasing in the requirements over the next two years. Implementation of the policy will be evaluated in 2015.

Realization of this policy by all Agency staff and in all of the countries in which we work will help to bring to fruition USAID's development vision of a world in which women and men, girls and boys enjoy economic, social, cultural, civil, and political rights and are equally empowered to secure better lives for themselves, their families, and their communities.

1 INTRODUCTION

Gender equality and female empowerment are now universally recognized as core development objectives, fundamental for the realization of human rights, and key to effective and sustainable development outcomes.[1]

No society can develop sustainably without increasing and transforming the distribution of opportunities, resources, and choices for males and females so that they have equal power to shape their own lives and contribute to their communities. A growing body of research demonstrates that societies with greater gender equality experience faster economic growth, and benefit from greater agricultural productivity and improved food security. Empowering women to participate in and lead public and private institutions makes these institutions more representative and effective. Increasing girls' and women's education and access to resources improves the health and education of the next generation. Women also play critical roles as effective peace advocates, community leaders, and champions of civil and human rights.

The 2010 Quadrennial Diplomacy and Development Review (QDDR), prepared jointly by the State Department and USAID, placed women at the center of U.S. diplomacy and development — not simply as beneficiaries, but also as agents of peace, reconciliation, development, growth, and stability. The first operational principle in the USAID Policy Framework 2011-2015 is "Promote Gender Equality and Female Empowerment." This policy on Gender Equality and

BOX 1: DEFINITIONS

Gender equality[2] concerns women and men, and it involves working with men and boys, women and girls to bring about changes in attitudes, behaviors, roles and responsibilities at home, in the workplace, and in the community. Genuine equality means more than parity in numbers or laws on the books; it means expanding freedoms and improving overall quality of life so that equality is achieved without sacrificing gains for males or females.

Female empowerment[3] is achieved when women and girls acquire the power to act freely, exercise their rights, and fulfill their potential as full and equal members of society. While empowerment often comes from within, and individuals empower themselves, cultures, societies, and institutions create conditions that facilitate or undermine the possibilities for empowerment.

Gender integration involves identifying, and then addressing, gender inequalities during strategy and project design, implementation, and monitoring and evaluation. Since the roles and power relations between men and women affect how an activity is implemented, it is essential that project managers address these issues on an ongoing basis.

---

[1] These commitments have been codified in the Beijing Platform for Action signed in 1995 at the Fourth World Conference on Women in Beijing, China, the Millennium Development Goals adopted by 189 governments in 2000, UN Security Council Resolution 1325 on Women, Peace, and Security (as well as subsequent related resolutions 1820, 1888, 1889, and 1960) and embodied in the Universal Declaration of Human Rights, among myriad other international treaties and declarations.
[2] Sex is the classification of people as male or female. At birth, infants are assigned a sex based on a combination of bodily characteristics including: chromosomes, hormones, internal reproductive organs and genitalia. Gender is the socially-defined set of roles, rights, responsibilities, entitlements, and obligations of females and males in societies. The social definitions of what it means to be female or male vary among cultures and change over time. Gender Identity is an individual's internal, personal sense of being male or female. For transgender people, their birth-assigned sex and their own internal sense of gender identity do not match.
[3] This policy deliberately uses the term "female" empowerment, as opposed to women's empowerment, to capture girls and adolescents. This differs from the organizational titles of USAID's Office of Gender Equality and Women's Empowerment, some Position Descriptions and usage in other USAID program and budget documents.

Female Empowerment seeks to codify and operationalize these principles across USAID policies and practices.

USAID's Experience Addressing Gender Equality and Female Empowerment

While USAID has a long history of addressing women's issues in development, accomplishments have been mixed and the intensity of the focus on gender issues has varied over time. In 1974, soon after passage of the 1973 Percy Amendment to the Foreign Assistance Act, USAID established the Women in Development (WID) Office to assist USAID missions and regional bureaus in integrating women into their various development projects.[4] A "Women in Development" Policy Paper was issued in 1982. It was supplemented in 1996 by a Gender Plan of Action (GPA) that included requirements for gender integration in policy, personnel, procurement, performance monitoring, and evaluation. An evaluation of the Plan in 2000 by the Advisory Committee on Voluntary Foreign Assistance (ACVFA) found a number of obstacles to effective institutionalization of the GPA, including large budget cuts coupled with expanding budget earmarks, disruptions caused by reorganization of U.S. foreign assistance agencies, low levels of consultation and communication about the Plan with Agency staff, and concern over proliferation of Agency priorities, among others.

Although few analyses have been carried out that allow for precise quantification of progress, one such analysis[5] revealed modest increases in the extent to which gender issues were integrated into country strategies over the period 1996-2005 and into procurement solicitations from May 2006 to February 2007. A second analysis of procurements[6] documented an improvement in the percentage of solicitations issued in 2010 that were scored as "moderate" to "thorough" on gender integration, as compared to 2006/7, and a decrease in the percentage of solicitations over the same time period that received the lowest possible score ("minimal").

Recently, greater progress has been made in integrating gender issues into Agency strategies, programs and procedures. In 2009, USAID revised its Automated Directives System (ADS), which contains Agency policy directives and mandatory procedures, to establish a more comprehensive approach to gender integration. Gender analysis is one of only two mandatory analysis requirements that are to be integrated in strategic planning, project design and approval, procurement processes, and measurement and evaluation. In 2011, the Agency reviewed and revised the technical competencies for different Foreign Service backstops to ensure that they reflect the knowledge, skills, and abilities that will be needed by technical officers to effectively address gender issues in their work. The Agency also introduced new definitions of gender issues for budget attributions in Operational Plans, along with a set of common indicators designed to

BOX 2:
FOSTERING WOMEN'S LEADERSHIP

In 2011, USAID significantly expanded efforts to support women's leadership in several fields. Anticipating release of the US National Action Plan on Women Peace and Security USAID provided financial support to meet the training, transportation, and security needs of female negotiators, and allocated funds to support the inclusion of women in high level decision-making processes, including formal peace negotiations, donor conferences, and transitional political processes. Complementary programs were created to cultivate women leaders in business, academia, and research; strengthen the skills of female legislators and legislative branch staff; foster women's leadership within social protection; and elevate women's leadership in the small- and medium-sized enterprise sector.

---

[4]The Percy Amendment, which is still in effect, requires U.S. bilateral assistance programs to enhance the integration of women into the national economies of developing countries, and instructs the State Department to consider progress on women's issues when making decisions about funding international organizations.
[5]DevTech, *Measuring Gender Integration in USAID Planning and Procurement,*" July 2007 (unpublished).
[6]DevTech, *Measuring Gender Integration in USAID Solicitation Documents Issued in 2010,* February 2011 (unpublished).

assess progress toward increasing gender equality and female empowerment (see Box 6). The Office of the Administrator and the Bureau for Policy, Planning and Learning (PPL) created two senior positions devoted exclusively to gender equality and female empowerment; the Office of Gender Equality and Women's Empowerment was renamed and upgraded; and the Bureau of Democracy, Conflict, and Humanitarian Assistance (DCHA) created a Center of Excellence on Democracy, Human Rights, and Governance with a particular focus on gender equality and women's rights. Finally, missions and offices began to scale up programs that work - expand coverage and access to medical and psycho-social care, legal assistance, and income generating activities for gender-based violence (GBV) survivors in the Democratic Republic of the Congo, and extend Safe Schools, an innovative program to reduce school-related gender-based violence, to the Dominican Republic, Senegal, Yemen, and Tajikistan, among others.

For these efforts to be accelerated and sustained, USAID needs a coherent, relevant, and up-to-date Agency policy on gender equality and female empowerment. The world has changed considerably since 1982, and the literature and field experience related to closing gender gaps has substantially expanded. This new policy on Gender Equality and Female Empowerment builds on this evidence base and the best practices of USAID and other donors, and provides an overarching framework for gender integration throughout all aspects of our work.

2 A GLOBAL SNAPSHOT OF GENDER EQUALITY AND FEMALE EMPOWERMENT IN 2012

A large body of evidence has established that gender inequality has costs for individuals and societies and these costs can multiply across generations.[7] For instance, women's economic dependency on men reduces their ability to exercise safer sex options to protect themselves against unwanted pregnancies and HIV infection.[8] When women cannot participate in the labor force, are prevented by law or practice from entering certain occupations, or excluded from management positions, GDP growth can suffer by as much as two percent.[9] Conversely, gender equality not only benefits individual males and females but whole sectors and societies. For instance, the Food and Agriculture Organization of the United Nations (FAO) estimates that if women had the same access to productive resources as men, they could increase yields on their farms by 20 to 30 percent, which in turn could raise total agricultural output in developing countries by 2.5 to 4 percent and reduce the number of hungry people in the world by 12 to 17 percent, up to 150 million people.[10]

Great strides have been made to reduce gender gaps and improve the status of women and girls over the past three decades. Yet, significant gender gaps remain across sectors in all countries around the world; they are often greater among the poor. Historically, gender inequalities have disadvantaged females, and while that remains the case in many domains, gender norms and policies also negatively affect boys and men in specific regions and sectors.

Education
Gender gaps in primary education have closed in the vast majority of developing countries since 2000. Progress has been particularly notable at the primary school level in the Arab States, South and West Asia and sub-Saharan Africa – the regions with the largest gender gaps in 2000. Still, in 2012, South Asia and West Africa continue to have large gender gaps that disfavor girls in primary education. In Afghanistan, Chad, and the Central African Republic, for instance, fewer than 70 girls per 100 boys are enrolled in primary school. On the other hand, boys are less likely to complete primary education than girls in 24 countries, including Lesotho, Nicaragua, Suriname, Namibia, Bangladesh, and Bhutan.

Progress is less evident at the secondary level: gender parity has not improved in sub-Saharan Africa or in the Arab States. In contrast, in many countries in Latin America and the Caribbean and Europe and Eurasia, girls have had higher attendance at secondary schools than boys since the mid-1980s. In countries in other regions, such as sub-Saharan Africa and South Asia, girls are often more likely to drop out of secondary school even when they have completed primary education.[11]

Progress in school entry has not been accompanied by changes in other domains. Fields of study, for instance, still tend to be segregated by sex, with more males choosing or being encouraged to pursue higher status and better paid careers in science, technology, and engineering while females predominate in the lower paying education, health care and social service professions.

Mortality and Reproductive Health
Over the past 30 years, huge strides have been made, particularly in life expectancy, fertility, and mortality. However, gender inequality continues to have a negative impact on a range of

---

[7]The World Bank, *World Development Report 2012: Gender Equality and Development*, (Washington, DC: The World Bank, 2011); online at *http://siteresources.worldbank.org/INTWDR2012/Resources/7778105-1299699968583/7786210-1315936222006/Complete-Report.pdf*.

[8]Ellen Weiss, Daniel Whelan, and Geeta Rao Gupta, "Gender, Sexuality and HIV: Making a Difference in the Lives of Young Women in Developing Countries." *Sexual and Relationship Therapy* 15(3) (2000): 233-245.

[9]The World Bank. *op cit.*

[10]Hafez Ghanem, *The State of Food and Agriculture 2010-11: Women in Agriculture: Closing the Gender Gap for Development*. (Rome: The Food and Agricultural Organization, 2011).

[11]UNESCO, *EFA Global Monitoring Report 2011: The Hidden Crisis: Armed Conflict and Education*. (Paris: UNESCO, 2011).

health issues. Gender-related power imbalances contribute to excess female mortality across the life cycle: at birth, during infancy and early childhood, and throughout the reproductive years. Harmful gender norms affect men and boys by encouraging risk-taking and by limiting their health-seeking behavior. In Russia, Ukraine, and other countries in Eurasia, the life expectancy of men has been dramatically reduced by substance abuse and other risky behaviors.

Although the reproductive health of women and girls has improved over the past few decades, more than 127 million women in sub-Saharan Africa and South Central Asia in 2010 still have an unmet need for modern contraceptives (215 million across all developing countries). Taking into account projected population growth, this number will increase to 176 million in the next two decades if concerns about the availability of contraceptive methods are not addressed.[12] Adolescent fertility rates also remain high; young women have higher unmet need for contraception and higher chances than older women of suffering from complications at birth. Maternal mortality is especially high in sub-Saharan Africa and parts of Asia, owing mainly to a failure to provide adequate family planning and maternity care to childbearing women. Maternal deaths in developing countries could be reduced by 70 percent, and newborn deaths cut nearly in half, if the world doubled its investment in family planning and maternal and newborn health care.[13]

Women are more vulnerable than men to sexually transmitted infections, particularly HIV/AIDS. Unequal gender norms often prevent men and women from seeking HIV testing, counseling, and treatment, as well as disclosing their HIV status. Today, women and girls make up almost half the infected population ages 15–49 worldwide; in sub-Saharan Africa the rate is close to 60 percent. The persistence of gender-based violence contributes to women's increased risk and vulnerability.

Gender-Based Violence

A range of evidence points to the high global prevalence of gender based violence (GBV) which in the broadest definition is violence directed at an individual based on his or her biological sex, gender identity, or perceived adherence to socially defined norms of masculinity and femininity.[14] GBV is a constraint to individual and societal development and has high human and economic costs. For instance, women who experience violence from their partners are less likely to earn a living and less able to care for their children. Children who witness violence are significantly more at risk for health problems, anxiety disorders, poor school performance and violent behavior. The economic effects of violence against women include increased absenteeism; decreased labor market participation; reduced productivity; lower earnings, investment, and savings; and lower intergenerational productivity.[15]

Population-based prevalence data for one form of GBV - intimate partner violence - now exists for more than 90 countries, although there are still some regions, such as the Middle East and West Africa, where data is relatively limited. The prevalence of physical or sexual violence experienced by women varies widely across countries. A ten-country study using Demographic and Health Survey (DHS) data of ever-married women reporting spousal/intimate partner violence shows rates ranging from 48 percent in Zambia, 44 percent in Colombia, and 42 percent in Peru, to 18 percent in Cambodia, 19 percent in India, and 22 percent in the Dominican Republic.[16] Intimate partner violence cuts across socioeconomic, religious, and ethnic groups and across geographic areas, but women living in poverty, women with disabilities, and adolescent girls are especially vulnerable.[17] At least 2 million girls are at risk of Female Genital Mutilation (FGM) each year in at least 28 countries, primarily in sub-Saharan Africa, but also northern Iraq, Malaysia, and Indonesia, exposing them to a wide range of health risks from incontinence to increased risk of childbirth complications and

---

[12]United Nations Population Division, *World Population Prospects, 2010 Revision*, (New York: United Nations Population Division, 2010).

[13]Susheela Singh et al., *Adding it Up: The Costs and Benefits of Investing in Family Planning and Maternal and Newborn Health* (New York: Guttmacher Institute and UNFPA, 2009).

[14]Gender-based violence includes physical, sexual, and psychological abuse; threats; coercion; arbitrary deprivation of liberty; and economic deprivation, whether in public or private life. Types of GBV include female infanticide; harmful traditional practices such as early and forced marriage, "honor" killings, and female genital cutting; child sexual abuse and slavery; trafficking in persons; sexual coercion and abuse; neglect; violence against lesbian, gay, bisexual, and transgender individuals; domestic violence; and elder abuse. It can occur throughout the lifecycle, from the prenatal phase through childhood and adolescence, the reproductive years, and old age (Claudia Garcia-Moreno et al., "Prevalence of Intimate Partner Violence: Findings from the WHO Multi-Country Study on Women's Health and Domestic Violence," *The Lancet* 368 (2006): 1260–69).

[15]Andrew Morrison and Maria Beatriz Orlando, *The Costs and Impacts of Gender-Based Violence in Developing Countries: Methodological Considerations and New Evidence* (Washington, DC: The World Bank, November 2004).

[16]Michelle Hindin, Sunita Kishor, and Donna Ansara, *Intimate Partner Violence among Couples in 10 DHS Countries: Predictors and Health Outcomes*, DHS Analytical Studies 18 (Washington, DC: USAID, December 2008). Accurate statistical data on the prevalence of gender-based violence are difficult to obtain because of underreporting by victims and underrecording by police, which also mean that existing evidence most likely underestimates prevalence.

[17]Charlotte Watts and Cathy Zimmerman, "Violence against Women: Global Scope and Magnitude," *The Lancet* 359 (2002): 1121-37.

newborn deaths.[18] While GBV disproportionately affects women and girls, men and boys also experience sexual violence, increasingly documented in conflict countries,[19] and especially when their gender identity conflicts with gender norms.

Paid Employment and Asset Ownership

Women's participation in the paid labor force in developing countries has grown in the past 30 years as expanding economic opportunities and economic necessity have drawn many female workers into the market. Countries that had low rates of female participation in 1980 – for instance in Latin America and the Caribbean and North Africa – saw dramatic increases. Female participation rates are greater than 50 percent in sub-Saharan Africa, East Asia and the Pacific, and Latin America and the Caribbean. The Middle East and North Africa and South Asia have the lowest female labor force participation rates.

Increased participation has not translated into equal employment opportunities or equal earnings for men and women. Women and men tend to work in very different parts of the economy with little change over time, even in higher income countries. In almost all countries, women are more likely than men to engage in low-productivity and labor-intensive activities. They are also more likely to be in unpaid family employment or work in the informal wage sector. In agriculture, especially in Africa, women operate smaller plots of land and farm less remunerative crops. Across all regions, as entrepreneurs, women tend to own and manage smaller firms (measured by sales, employment, and assets) and to concentrate in less-profitable sectors. As a result of these differences, gender gaps in earnings and productivity persist across sectors and forms of economic activity, including wage employment and entrepreneurship.[20]

Although country-level data is limited, women in developing countries are far less likely than men to own or control key productive assets like land and housing. Researchers in 2003 found that women represented only one-third or less of landowners in the five Latin American countries they examined.[21] In the Europe and Eurasia region, land privatization schemes after the fall of communism resulted in many more men than women being granted titles to land. More recently, the World Bank's *World Development Report 2012* cites data from 16 countries in 5 developing regions showing that female-headed households are far less likely to own land. And across all developing regions, female land holdings are systematically smaller than male landholdings, and the mean value of men's landholdings is substantially larger than that of women's, controlling for socioeconomic and other factors.

Demographic Shifts and Time Use

Women's increased participation in paid employment and public life has a number of implications for time use and care of dependents. Around the world, women devote more time each day to housework and care of children, the elderly, the disabled, and other dependents than their male partners; differences range from 1 to 3 hours more for housework and 2 to 10 times more time for care of children, the elderly, and the sick, leaving women and girls with 1 to 4 hours less time each day than men and boys for market or other productive activities.[22] Even as women have entered the paid labor force, they remain largely responsible for care and housework. These patterns are accentuated after marriage and childbearing.

In addition, declining mortality rates are likely to exacerbate these pressures on women. Unlike in developed countries, where social security, elderly day care, housing for the elderly, and comprehensive medical care help the elderly live a more independent lifestyle, similar services do not exist in most developing countries. This implies that, unless gender norms change and unpaid work is reduced and redistributed between men and women, more and more females in the developing world will be expected to care for aging parents in addition to their child care and income-earning responsibilities.

Participation, Governance, and Legal Rights

Women's representation in national legislatures and local governments has increased during the past two decades. For example, women's share of seats in national legislatures

---

[18]The prevalence of FGM varies significantly from country to country, from nearly 98 percent in Somalia to less than one percent in Uganda. New evidence shows prevalence in other countries including Yemen, Iran, Syria, Oman, and Saudi Arabia. See World Health Organization, *Female Genital Mutilation*, (Geneva: World Health Organization, February 2010). Online at www.who.int/mediacentre/factsheets/fs241/en/index.html.

[19]Kiersten Johnson et al., "Association of Sexual Violence and Human Rights Violations with Physical and Mental Health in Territories of the Eastern Democratic of the Congo," *JAMA* 304(5) (2010).

[20]In almost all countries, women in manufacturing earn less than men. In agriculture, farms operated by women on average have lower yields than those operated by men, even for men and women in the same households and for men and women cultivating the same crops. Female entrepreneurs are also less productive than male entrepreneurs because of industry/occupational segregation and lower access to credit and productive inputs, and not because they are inherently less efficient.

[21]Carmen Diana Deere and Magdalena León, "The Gender Asset Gap: Land in Latin America," *World Development* 31(6) (2003): 925-47.

[22]World Bank *op cit*

increased from 10 percent to 17 percent worldwide between 1995 and 2009, and all but 1 of the 10 countries without women's suffrage in 1980 have since granted women the right to vote. Still, in 2011, women held only 19.4 percent of the seats in lower and upper houses of parliaments globally.[23] To redress imbalances, 104 countries currently have provisions to promote women's representation in legislatures at the national or sub-national level; for instance India, Bangladesh, Pakistan and Nepal reserve 33 percent of legislative seats for women at the municipal and district levels. Women also remain considerably underrepresented in other political bodies, holding less than one-fifth of all cabinet positions worldwide. Furthermore, despite numeric gains, the quality of women's participation in political affairs is often lacking due to a variety of constraints including lower levels of political experience and access to mentoring.

Research has found that higher numbers of women in legislative bodies increases the attention to gender equality in legislation and budgets.[24] Nonetheless, in many countries, key areas of women's rights are neither recognized nor protected; for instance, in parts of sub-Saharan Africa, South Asia, and the Middle East, women lack independent rights to own land, manage property, conduct business or even travel without their husband's consent.[24] Although many countries have taken steps to reform marital and property rights laws, the implementation and enforcement of new legislation is inconsistent.

In the realm of peace-building, women are severely marginalized. In major peace processes since 1992, women constituted fewer than 3 percent of mediators and 8 percent of negotiators, numbers that have not markedly improved since the passage over a decade ago of the landmark UN Security Council Resolution 1325 recognizing the central role of women in conflict prevention, peace processes and peacebuilding. Furthermore, women are a similarly limited share of the participants in decision-making forums related to transition planning and post-conflict reconstruction such as donor conferences convened to allocate resources for post-conflict recovery.

Crisis, Conflict and Natural Disasters

As the nature of crises and conflicts have changed over the past decades so too have the roles of men and women and the ways they are affected. Forced displacement exposes refugees and internally-displaced persons, especially women and girls, to additional risks and exploitation. Violence against women, especially rape, sexual assault, abduction, mutilation, forced prostitution and sexual slavery, is a facet of many recent conflicts from the Balkans to sub-Saharan Africa, the Middle East and Central Asia.[25]

Unfortunately, post-conflict peacebuilding, recovery, and disarmament, demobilization and reintegration (DDR) programs do not always recognize the complex roles females and males play during conflict, as combatants, forced laborers, and sex slaves. Following conflict, a narrow set of stakeholders usually shapes, implements and is served by post-conflict recovery programs. For example, DDR programs often fail to differentiate between the needs of male and female combatants in their design. They also tend to underestimate and underserve boys and girls who were child soldiers. Moreover, critical issues are often overlooked; for example, of 300 ceasefire accords, power-sharing arrangements and other peace agreements negotiated since 1989, just 18 of them – only 6 percent – contain even a passing reference to sexual violence. The growth of women's participation in peace processes and post-conflict transitions in countries ranging from Kosovo to Liberia is helping to ensure that peace agreements and reconstruction address more comprehensively the issues that need to be resolved to achieve lasting and just peace.[26]

During and following natural disasters, women and girls often suffer disproportionately due to socially-constructed norms, breakdowns in law and order, or disrupted livelihoods due to displacement. For example, up to four times as many females as males were killed in the 2004 Indian Ocean tsunami due to gender norms, such as women and girls' traditionally not being taught how to swim. Following the 2010 Haiti earthquake, human trafficking of women and girls increased dramatically while sexual assaults in relief camps posed a significant problem.

---

[23]Inter-Parliamentary Union, accessed January 2012, http://www.ipu.org/wmn-e/world.htm. For comparison, women held only 16.8 percent of seats in the U.S. Congress in 2011.

[24]Raghabendra Chattopadhyay and Esther Duflo, "Women as Policy Makers: Evidence from a Randomized Policy Experiment in India." *Econometrica* 72 (5) (2004): 1409–43.

[25]Donald Steinberg, "Women and War: An Agenda for Action" in *Women and War: Power and Protection in the 21st Century*, ed. Kuehnast et al., (Washington, DC: US Institute for Peace, 2011).

[26]United States National Action Plan on Women, Peace, and Security, 2011.

3 USAID'S VISION AND GOAL

USAID's development vision is a world in which women and men, girls and boys enjoy economic, social, cultural, civil, and political rights and are equally empowered to secure better lives for themselves, their families, and their communities; are equally able to access quality education and health-care; accumulate and control their own economic assets and resources; exercise their own voice, and live free from intimidation, harassment, discrimination, and violence. Responsibilities for earning income and the care of family members are not restricted by the roles or stereotypes society has defined for males and females. Women and men, girls and boys treat each other with mutual respect and dignity and participate freely and equally in economic and political decision-making at the regional, national and local levels. Women's and girls' unique expertise, initiatives, leadership, and contributions are recognized and supported by individuals and governments, leading to their economic, social, and political empowerment.

USAID seeks to improve the lives of citizens around the world by advancing equality between women and girls and men and boys, and empowering women and girls to participate fully in and benefit from the development of their societies.

4 OUTCOMES

USAID investments are aimed at achieving three overarching outcomes for all people. These outcomes are especially important for males and females who are marginalized or excluded due to ethnicity, gender identity, sexual orientation, lack of income, disability, or other factors. They reflect the gamut of activities that USAID can undertake across multiple sectors and fields to achieve the goal of this policy:

Reduce gender disparities in access to, control over and benefit from resources, wealth, opportunities, and services — economic, social, political, and cultural.

Reduce gender-based violence and mitigate its harmful effects on individuals and communities, so that all people can live healthy and productive lives.

Increase capability of women and girls to realize their rights, determine their life outcomes, and influence decision-making in households, communities, and societies.

These outcomes are deliberately set at a general level. However, in strategic planning and project design at the country or sub-national level, they should be adapted into specific results that have associated targets and indicators for tracking progress. For instance, in a food security strategy, the first outcome could be operationalized as "Reduce the gap between female and male farmers' access to productive inputs and services (credit, seeds, new technology, and agricultural extension) by 25 percent." Indicators like the Women's Empowerment in Agriculture Index should be used to track progress toward this specific result in different country contexts. Further discussion of these options will be provided in forthcoming Implementation Guidance.

 # OPERATIONAL PRINCIPLES OF THE GENDER EQUALITY AND FEMALE EMPOWERMENT POLICY

The following principles underpin USAID's commitment to empowerment, protection, and participation of males and females in their societies.[27] They also reflect the principles in USAID Policy Framework 2011-2015, draw on the reform agenda identified in *USAID Forward*, are consistent with key points made in the QDDR, and were developed in conjunction with other related USAID policies, specifically the 2012 Counter-Trafficking in Persons Policy and forthcoming Youth in Development Policy (see Box 3).

Integrate gender equality and female empowerment into USAID's work: This policy will be implemented by integrating approaches and actions to advance gender equality and female empowerment throughout the Program Cycle — in Agency-level policy and strategy formulation; Country Development Cooperation Strategies (CDCS); project design and implementation; and monitoring, evaluation, and learning.

The identification of specific gender equality and female empowerment results to be achieved is based on the findings of gender analyses, which are mandated by the ADS for country strategies and projects (see Box 4), and by other relevant analyses that may be used in the context of strategic planning and programming. Gender equality and empowerment of women and girls cannot be achieved without considering the socio-cultural context in which males and females live. Working with men and boys to understand the importance of girls' education, and women's employment and career aspirations, for example, is fundamental to bringing about sustainable and transformational social change. At the same time, men and boys are faced with different challenges and vulnerabilities imposed on them by rigid definitions of masculinity. Societal expectations narrow male roles so working with men and boys to reframe broader definitions of masculinity can expand their own range of

BOX 3:
USAID POLICIES ON COUNTER-TRAFFICKING IN PERSONS AND YOUTH IN DEVELOPMENT

Trafficking in Persons (TIP) is a crime that involves either sex or labor exploitation, or both. At its essence, TIP is about people being bought and sold as property. Estimates in 2010 of the number of people enslaved in sex or labor exploitation range from 12 to 27 million. Trafficking can impede efforts to improve health, to increase economic growth, to achieve gender equality and women's empowerment, and poses a threat to lifetime prospects for youth. USAID's new Counter-Trafficking in Persons Policy empowers the Agency to redouble efforts to remain a thought and action leader working towards a world in which human beings are no longer bought and sold.

In 2012, USAID is also adopting a new Youth in Development Policy that outlines how USAID can strategically support, protect, prepare, and engage young people in achieving development outcomes. The Youth in Development and Gender Equality and Female Empowerment policies are closely aligned in recognizing that gender norms determine the way households allocate resources to sons and daughters, through decisions about boys' or girls' education, where they work, and how they spend their time. A large body of evidence shows that intervening early in key areas – to raise the age of marriage, provide HIV/AIDS information and services, and reduce gender-based violence – can have long-term payoffs for girls, their households, and broader communities.

---

[27]USAID is also "walking the walk" by ensuring that women are recruited for entry into the Civil and Foreign Service, empowered to contribute fully to our development mission, given opportunities through mentorships, treated fairly in the promotion/evaluation/assignment processes, and challenged to lead our Agency.

BOX 4:
GENDER ANALYSIS

The ADS requires staff to conduct a gender analysis in the design of country strategies and projects, which must in turn be reflected in associated project appraisal documents, Statements of Work (SOWs)/Program Descriptions and Requests for Applications (RFAs)/Requests for Proposals (RFPs). Gender analysis is a tool for examining the differences between the roles that women and men play in communities and societies, the different levels of power they hold, their differing needs, constraints and opportunities, and the impact of these differences on their lives.

At the strategy and project level, the gender analysis should identify root causes of existing gender inequalities or obstacles to female empowerment in that context so that USAID can proactively address them in the project design and seek out opportunities to promote women's leadership and participation. The gender analysis should also identify potential adverse impacts and/or risks of gender-based exclusion that could result from planned activities, including: (a) Displacing women from access to resources or assets; (b) Increasing the unpaid work or caregiver burden of females relative to males; (c) Conditions that restrict the participation of women or men in project activities and benefits based on pregnancy, maternity/paternity leave, or marital status; (d) Increasing the risk of gender-based violence, including sexual exploitation or human trafficking, sexually transmitted diseases, and HIV/AIDS; and (e) Marginalizing or excluding women in political and governance processes. Because males and females are not homogenous groups, gender analysis should also to the extent possible disaggregate by income, region, caste, race, ethnicity, disability, and other relevant social characteristics and explicitly recognize the specific needs of young girls and boys, adolescent girls and boys, adult women and men, and older women and men.

opportunities. All society will benefit when harmful gender norms are eliminated.

While integrating gender equality and female empowerment into USAID's strategic planning and project design processes will improve sustainable development outcomes, this alone does not ensure that the Agency is addressing the most critical gender gaps in particular contexts or directing resources where they are most needed to empower females. Therefore, Missions may also develop specific gender equality Development Objectives (DOs) and all Operating Units (OUs) may invest in stand-alone projects that are determined to be strategic to the achievement of gender equality and female empowerment. These DOs and related interventions will depend on the specific country context, but should be scalable and innovative, and designed to link to broader sectoral and country programming.

Pursue an inclusive approach to foster equality: This

policy is inclusive of all women and men, girls and boys, regardless of age, sexual orientation, gender identity, disability status, religion, ethnicity, socioeconomic status, geographic area, migratory status, forced displacement, or HIV/AIDS status. In each country context, USAID will address gender gaps across the human life cycle, recognizing that the precise nature and impact of gender inequality changes as people age and assume new roles in their families and communities. Closing gender gaps in adolescence is particularly important since gender inequalities in education, time use, and health can accumulate across the life cycle if not broken early (see Box 3).[28] USAID will also be aware of the diversity of households and family structures, which requires particular attention to domestic partners, child-headed households, single-person households formed by older adults, and the presence of secondary families formed by single parents within extended households. This inclusive focus will ensure that key gender gaps are reduced in ways that benefit all citizens, not just those who are the most visible, vocal, or who may have the easiest access to USAID programming.

---

[28]World Bank *op cit* and Ruth Levine et al., *Girls Count: A Global Investment and Action Agenda* (Washington, DC: Center for Global Development, 2009).

Build partnerships across a wide range of stakeholders:
USAID will partner with a wide range of key actors to ensure that our efforts to increase gender equality and female empowerment are coordinated and non-duplicative, and reflect country priorities. This includes host governments; international and host country civil society; women's organizations; the donor community, foundations; lesbian, gay, bisexual and transgender advocates; and the private sector, including women-led businesses. USAID's partnerships with local individuals and organizations will capitalize on and leverage their passion, experience, and achievements, while building their capacity as advocates, leaders, and voices for change.

BOX 5:
USING SCIENCE AND TECHNOLOGY

In February 2011, USAID and AusAID launched a partnership with GSMA, the leading mobile phone operators association, to reduce by half the mobile phone gender gap of 300 million in the developing world. The mWomen Partnership identifies what women look for when deciding whether to adopt mobile services and how these services can promote greater opportunities and empowerment. The three-year program includes technical assistance grants to mobile operators to help them implement mWomen opportunities and products; support for NGOs to work with mobile operators and design activities that address the barriers to mobile usage by women; research into women's wants and needs, such as within mobile financial services; and focused attention on maximizing the benefits from mobile phone use, including financial inclusion, education and healthcare.

The Global Alliance for Clean Cookstoves, a public-private partnership to save lives, improve livel hoods, empower women, and combat climate change, seeks to create a thriving global market for clean and efficient household cooking solutions. Through the alliance, USAID supports applied and operational research into how people use improved stove technology and how indoor air quality and sanitation interventions can improve household environments and promote economic opportunities for women.

Crucial to the success of this policy in fulfilling the mandates of the Presidential Policy Directive on Global Development and the QDDR is close collaboration with other relevant offices within U.S. Government departments and agencies, especially the State Department's Office of Global Women's Issues (S/GWI). Inter-agency cooperation facilitates attention to gender equality and women's empowerment in U.S. defense, diplomatic, and development efforts, and augments the impact of each agency's own programming.

Harness science, technology, and innovation to reduce gender gaps and empower women and girls: USAID interventions to promote gender equality and female empowerment should make bold, imaginative, and creative use of new technologies and innovations that hold great promise for increasing men's and women's health and well-being. For instance, high tech tools such as the internet and cell phones, as well as low tech innovations such as clean cookstoves, have the power to improve women's safety and health, increase economic productivity, and reduce unpaid labor (see Box 5). Scientific research and development of microbicides can both prevent the transmission of HIV/AIDS and manage fertility. Using science and technology to help change social norms and stereotypes can help reduce gender disparities.

Address the unique challenges in crisis and conflict-affected environments: USAID's work in crisis, conflict-affected, and fragile states will facilitate women's participation in peace processes and decision-making, promote women's roles in conflict prevention and recovery, strengthen its efforts to prevent and protect women from gender-based violence, ensure that relief and recovery efforts are specifically responsive to the different needs and priorities of women and men, and enable women's safe and equitable access to assistance, services, and livelihood support. Consistent with Executive Order 13595 and the accompanying U.S. Government 2011 National Action Plan on Women, Peace and Security, USAID, along with the State Department and Department of Defense, will have an implementation plan on women, peace and security that specifies actions to be used to empower women as equal partners in preventing conflict and building peace and increase the protection of women and girls in situations of conflict and insecurity. Through realization of the plan, USAID will be better able to capitalize on the unique roles of women and girls in conflict and crisis situations while better ensuring that they are effectively protected and assisted when faced with insecurity.

Serve as a thought-leader and a learning community: USAID will measure performance in closing key gender gaps and empowering women and girls. Monitoring and evaluation methods should include indicators that measure progress toward gender equality and women's empowerment (see Box 6 for the list of gender equality, women's empowerment, and gender-based violence indicators in the State-USAID Standardized Foreign Assistance Framework) and projects should collect and use sex-disaggregated data. Becoming a learning community means that USAID will work actively to learn from successes and failures and distill, showcase, and circulate throughout the Agency best practices on gender integration and achieving results that reduce gender gaps and empower women and girls.

Hold ourselves accountable: Promoting gender equality and female empowerment is a shared Agency responsibility and depends on the contribution and collective commitment of all staff. Senior managers, Mission Directors, and others will be held accountable for implementing this policy in bureau and mission portfolios and for defining concrete quantitative and qualitative results in strategies that are consistent with the outcomes outlined in Section 5 above. Specific responsibilities are spelled out in detail in the next section.

BOX 6:
BECOMING A LEARNING COMMUNITY:
GENDER EQUALITY AND FEMALE EMPOWERMENT INDICATORS

In 2011, the State-USAID Performance Plan & Report system was significantly revised and the entire Foreign Assistance (FA) indicator suite was reengineered. Consistent with the Outcomes described in Section 4 of this policy, the new system includes seven output and outcome indicators on gender equality, female empowerment, and gender-based violence that should be used in Performance Management Plans for tracking progress toward implementation results and measuring impact across programs:

- Number of laws, policies, or procedures drafted, proposed, or adopted to promote gender equality at the regional, national or local level.

- Proportion of female participants in USG-assisted programs designed to increase access to productive economic resources (assets, credit, income, or employment).

- Proportion of females who report increased self-efficacy at the conclusion of USG-supported training/ programming.

- Proportion of target population reporting increased agreement with the concept that males and females should have equal access to social, economic, and political opportunities.

- Number of laws, policies or procedures drafted, proposed, or adopted with USG assistance designed to improve prevention of or response to gender-based violence at the regional, national, or local level.

- Number of people reached by a USG-funded intervention providing GBV services (e.g., health, legal, psycho-social counseling, shelters, hotlines, other).

- Percentage of target population that views gender-based violence as less acceptable after participating in or being exposed to USG programming.

Becoming a learning agency involves more than using these indicators to report whether USAID programming is having the intended results. It also involves investments in rigorous monitoring and evaluation that collects appropriate sex-disaggregated data, asks clear questions about male and female roles and impacts to uncover intended and unintended positive and negative impacts, develops indicators designed to track changes in key gender gaps from baseline to endline, and uses rigorous qualitative and quantitative methodologies.

6 ORGANIZATIONAL ROLES AND RESPONSIBILITIES

This policy applies to all bureaus and missions and covers policy and operations in Washington and the field. In order to institutionalize this policy, missions and bureaus will carry out the following roles and responsibilities.

Missions, Regional Missions, and Country Offices will:

Adopt or revise, and periodically update, a Mission Order (MO) on Gender that: describes how the mission will implement the Agency's Gender Equality and Female Empowerment policy, including: integrating gender equality and female empowerment objectives throughout the Program Cycle; ensuring that the three Gender Sub-Key Issues are reflected in budget attributions in Operating Plans (OPs); ensuring that appropriate gender indicators are reported in Performance Plans and Reports (PPRs); assigning specific and detailed roles and responsibilities to mission staff; and ensuring that all staff who are required to do so receive gender training (see Section 7 below).

Hold implementing partners responsible for integrating gender into programming, developing indicators that measure specific gender equality goals for each activity, and consistently reporting to USAID on results related to gender equality and female empowerment.

Through the Program Office, provide data to Regional Bureau Program Offices and Gender Advisors to incorporate into regional reports on gender attributions in OPs, PPRs, and other required reporting, and address any problems revealed by these analyses. As part of the Program Performance Plan and Report, provide feedback and lessons learned on implementation of this policy.

Appoint a Mission Gender Advisor. The Gender Advisor should have (or be given the opportunity to fully develop) the technical skills and competencies necessary to provide appropriate guidance to technical and program staff to ensure that the policy is successfully implemented at the mission. Missions will determine the appropriate personnel category (e.g., FSO, FSN, PSC) for the Gender Advisor position, whether the position will be full- or part-time, and to whom the incumbent will report. Small missions, to be identified by regional bureaus through a consultative process (explained in forthcoming Implementation Guidance), or those in the process of closing are exempted from the requirement to have a Gender Advisor, but should nonetheless designate a staff member to serve as a point of contact for AID/W on issues related to this policy. Gender Advisors in regional missions will provide support to small missions. In all cases, the advisor will have responsibilities explicitly included in their job description, with an estimate of time allocation to carry out the work.

Be accountable, through the Mission Director, for implementation of the Gender Equality and Female Empowerment policy in mission portfolios and staff performance plans.

Regional Bureaus will:

Be the primary liaison between Washington, DC and Mission Gender Advisors.

Assist and support mission Program and Technical Offices and Gender Advisors, as needed, in conducting gender analyses related to country strategic planning and project design and integration of the results of these analyses into CDCS's, multi-year sector strategies, and project designs.

Keep missions apprised of key gaps, obstacles, research, and innovative programming approaches related to increasing gender equality and female empowerment that are appropriate for the specific region or countries within the region by sharing, responding to, or issuing relevant studies, tools, toolkits, reports, and evaluations.

Ensure that gender equality and female empowerment objectives are integrated into the bureau's regional programming, and that solicitations and contracts that are awarded reflect the mandated gender analyses.

Convey to regional bureau implementing partners the policy's requirements and provide appropriate oversight to ensure that all implementers comply with these requirements.

Ensure that gender issues are incorporated into all training programs organized by the regional bureau.

Work with missions to track attributions to gender sub-key issues in key planning documents such as OPs and PPRs and synthesize the data for the region into regional tables that PPL can use in the annual report to key stakeholders.

Ensure that regional bureau technical officers carry out gender analyses and integrate the findings into project designs and solicitations.

Ensure that regional bureau program officers monitor technical teams' adherence to gender integration in all phases of the programming cycle.

Have at least one Gender Advisor with regional expertise and appropriate technical and programmatic competency to provide guidance to regional bureaus technical and program staff to ensure that the policy is successfully implemented and to serve as primary bureau representative in Agencywide deliberations around gender issues. Gender Advisor(s) should have responsibilities explicitly included in their job description.

Through AAs, DAAs, and office directors, ensure accountability for implementation of the Gender Equality and Female Empowerment policy in bureau portfolios and work responsibilities of staff.

Pillar Bureaus will:

Provide guidance, including through the Policy's Implementation Guidance, on how gender equality and female empowerment can be advanced or achieved in technical sectors (e.g., Democracy, Human Rights and Governance, Economic Growth, Environment, Global Health, Agriculture, etc.).

Develop tools and toolkits on best practices for gender integration in each technical sector context.

Coordinate with regional bureaus to liaise with and provide support to mission Gender Advisors as pertinent to technical areas.

Ensure that gender issues are incorporated into all training programs offered by the pillar bureau.

Ensure that gender equality and female empowerment are reflected in the bureau's programming, solicitations, contracts and grants, and included as one dimension in the bureau portfolio reviews.

Convey to pillar bureau implementing partners the policy's requirements and provide appropriate oversight to ensure that all implementers comply with these requirements.

Ensure that pillar bureau technical officers carry out gender analyses and incorporate the findings from these analyses into project designs and resulting solicitations.

Ensure that pillar bureau program officers monitor technical teams' adherence to gender integration in all phases of the programming cycle.

Have at least one Gender Advisor with appropriate sector expertise and technical and programmatic competency to provide guidance to technical and program staff to ensure that the policy is successfully implemented and to serve as primary bureau representative in Agency-wide deliberations around gender issues. Gender Advisor(s) should have responsibilities explicitly included in their job description.

Through AAs, DAAs, and office directors, ensure accountability for implementation of the Gender Equality and Female Empowerment policy in bureau portfolios and work responsibilities of staff.

The Office of Gender Equality and Women's Empowerment (GenDev) will:

Manage centrally funded technical assistance and gender training contracts.

Provide targeted and strategic support to the Bureau of Economic Growth, Agriculture and Trade (EGAT).

Pilot innovative programs aimed at gender equality and female empowerment consistent with the mandate of the EGAT Bureau and advance/scale up successes through the regular program cycle.

Backstop regional bureau Gender Advisors to provide technical assistance on gender integration for missions, as needed.

Coordinate working groups for cross-sector issues such as gender-based violence and women's leadership programming.

Develop a repository of best practices on gender integration including topics related to gender analysis, project design, implementation, and evaluation and monitoring.

Coordinate knowledge management on gender integration through the Agency's webpage on gender equality and female empowerment.

Coordinate with the Office of Human Resources and other bureaus as appropriate to identify opportunities for training or develop in-house curriculum on gender (see Section 7 below), and support missions and AID/W operating units in delivering the training.

The Office of Acquisition and Assistance (OAA) will:

Require contract and agreement officers to perform due diligence to ensure that the results of gender analyses are clearly reflected in all solicitation documents (e.g., Statement of Work/Program Descriptions, project deliverables, key personnel requirements, and monitoring and evaluation requirements).

The Office of the General Counsel and Regional Legal Advisors will:

Ensure that bureaus and missions comply with ADS gender integration requirements in documents cleared by GC (PADs, PIOs, IAAs, and new contract actions, such as IQCs and LWAs).

Serve as a resource for bureau and mission staff to answer questions on ADS compliance and policy implementation.

Provide advice to PPL and other relevant offices regarding revisions to ADS requirements related to gender equality and women's empowerment.

The Office of Human Resources (HR) will:

Periodically review and revise required competencies in the positions for Foreign Service backstops, civil service employees, and Foreign Service Nationals to ensure that they reflect the knowledge, skills, and abilities that will be needed by technical and program officers to implement this policy.

Develop, in concert with PPL, GenDev, and other bureaus as appropriate, the competencies necessary for Gender Advisors.

Encourage supervisors to ensure that employees receive the training necessary to meet the standards for the gender competencies in their backstop or job series.

Encourage supervisors to use incentives such as on-the-spot and time off awards, Meritorious Honor Awards, Special Act Awards, and Certificates of Appreciation to recognize accomplishments in gender integration.

Coordinate with GenDev and other bureaus, as appropriate, to identify opportunities for training or develop in-house training (online, on-the-job, sector or other) for staff (see Section 7 below).

Monitor and seek to ensure a positive climate for women in the Agency.

---

[29]Formerly the Bureau for Economic Growth, Agriculture and Trade.

Bureau for Policy, Planning and Learning (PPL) will:

Ensure that gender equality and female empowerment objectives and results are incorporated into Agency-wide policies and strategies, and provide appropriate guidance for gender integration within Country Development Cooperation Strategies, project design, and learning and evaluation products.

Ensure that gender equality and female empowerment objectives and results are incorporated into all PPL-led training processes (e.g., Program Cycle, project design, monitoring and evaluation, and others).

Coordinate with the Office of Budget and Resource Management and regional and pillar bureau Program Offices to prepare an annual review of: 1) FY OPs to verify that relevant budget allocations are being attributed to the gender sub-key issues; and 2) PPRs to determine the extent to which results in advancing gender equality and women's empowerment objectives are being achieved.

Represent the Agency in high level donor and policy forums, such as the OECD GenderNet.

Have a formally-designated permanent and full-time Senior Gender Advisor, who will work in concert with relevant offices to ensure gender integration in policies and strategies and that reporting requirements are met.

The Office of the Administrator will:

Ensure sufficient resources are available to carry out the functions of the Policy.

Use the power of the Office to highlight the importance of gender equality and female empowerment as key development objectives.

Reach out to governments, civil society, and Congress to explain and stress the importance of gender equality and female empowerment in development assistance.

Represent the Agency in key USG interagency and policy forums.

Have a formally-designated permanent and full-time Senior Coordinator on Gender Equality and Women's Empowerment, who spearheads enhancement of U.S. development assistance efforts to serve and empower women and ensure gender equality goals are met.

7 AGENCY REQUIREMENTS

Successful implementation of this policy will require changes to Agency directives and procedures, as well as changes to Agency culture and practices. This section outlines additional Agency requirements for fulfilling the letter and spirit of the policy.

Automated Directives System (ADS):

- The ADS will incorporate specific guidance, roles, and responsibilities for conducting the mandatory gender analyses and for incorporating the findings of these analyses across the Program Cycle; attributing funds to the gender sub-key issues in the development of annual OPs; and using the gender equality indicators in annual PPRs.

Reporting

- In coordination with the S/GWI Office and Office of U.S. Foreign Assistance Resources (F), PPL will prepare an annual report on the Gender Equality marker for the OECD-DAC, beginning in 2012.[30]

- PPL, with the Senior Coordinator for Gender Equality and Women's Empowerment, will report annually on the results of the Agency's efforts to advance gender equality and female empowerment, beginning in 2013.

Training

- HR and GenDev will oversee the development of basic gender training for the Agency. Basic training on gender equality and female empowerment is required for (a) all Agency staff who design, evaluate or manage strategies and projects; (b) Agency staff (including Mission and OU Directors and Deputy Directors) who directly or indirectly supervise staff who design, evaluate or manage strategies and projects, (c) all Contracting and Assistance Officers, and (d) program officers. The Agency's goal is for all new staff to receive basic training within two years of their start date and for all other staff captured in categories (a) through (d) who have not had gender training, to receive training within two years.

- Similar to training for other competencies, advanced training should be instituted for all Gender Advisors and gender points of contact.

Human Resources Practices

- The Agency will use the existing awards system and other incentives to recognize gender champions in Washington and missions who demonstrate exemplary efforts to promote gender integration and to achieve the goals of this policy.

- The PPL Senior Gender Advisor will convene an Agency-wide community of practice to facilitate learning across offices and issues. GenDev will facilitate communities of practice on cross-sector issues such as Gender–Based Violence and Women's Leadership.

Implementation Guidance and Frequently Asked Questions will follow approval of this policy. The Implementation Guidance will include model Mission Orders, templates for conducting required gender analyses, model position descriptions for Gender Advisors, guidance for training, and a timetable for missions and USAID/W for phasing in the requirements of this policy over the next two years.

---

[30]The OECD-DAC marker system facilitates monitoring and co-ordination of Member States' activities in support of policy objectives for aid and covers the areas of economic well-being, social development, environment sustainability and regeneration and democratic accountability. The Gender Equality Marker is used by Member States to assess development interventions in terms of the contribution they make to gender equality and strengthening the rights of women.

In 2015, USAID will assess the implementation of this policy using appropriate performance benchmarks such as: gender integration in the results frameworks of Country Development Cooperation Strategies; an increase in the budget attributions to gender equality, women's empowerment, and gender-based violence in Operational Plans; use of the gender equality indicators in Performance Plans, and Reports; and increased gender integration in procurements and solicitations.

Conclusion

Gender equality and female empowerment are essential for achieving our development goals. Unless both women and men are able to attain their social, economic and political aspirations, and contribute to and shape decisions about the future, the global community will not successfully promote peace and prosperity. Realizing this policy in all of the countries in which we work will enable USAID to be a catalytic force for gender equality and women's empowerment worldwide and bring to fruition the vision of a world in which all people are equally empowered to secure better lives for themselves, their families, and their communities.

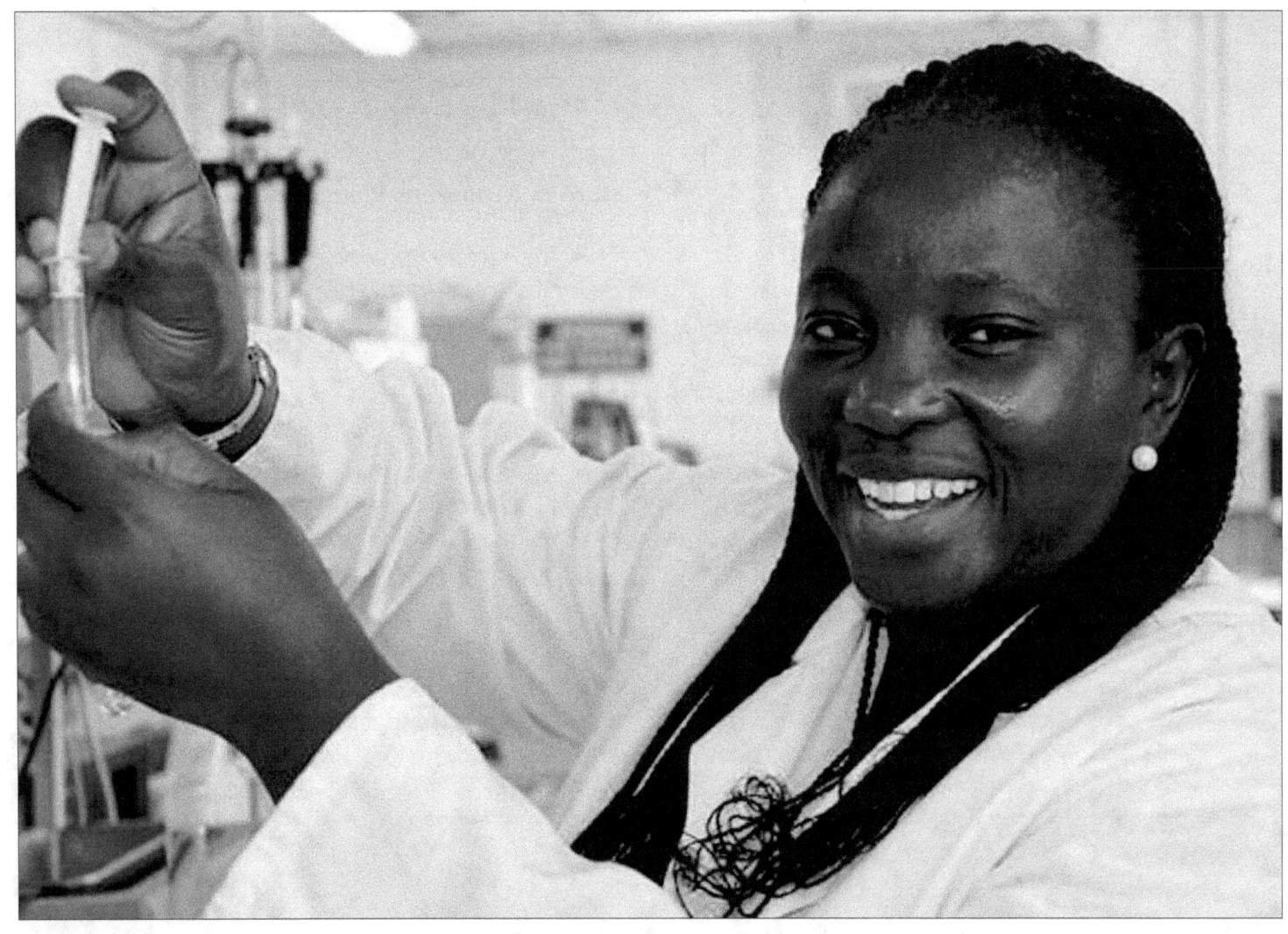